Jackson County Library Services
Medford, OR 97501

EAGLE
POINT

√10/03

Date Due

FEB 24 00			
JAN 07 99			
JUL 23			
OCT 17 00			
JAN 29 01			
JUN 30 01			
MAR 15 0			
NOV 27 0			
FEB 7 02			

WITHDRAWN
Damaged, Obsolete, or Surplus
Jackson County Library Services

12/98

Jackson
 County
  Library
   Services

HEADQUARTERS
413 W.Main
Medford, Oregon 97501

11-99

D1165114

LEADERS OF THE NORTH AND SOUTH

CIVIL WAR CHRONICLES

LEADERS OF THE NORTH AND SOUTH

BILL SELL

WITHDRAWN
Damaged, Obsolete, or Surplus
Jackson County Library Services

MetroBooks

JACKSON COUNTY
LIBRARY SERVICES
MEDFORD, OR 97501

An Imprint of Friedman/Fairfax Publishers

© 1996 by Michael Friedman Publishing Group, Inc.

All rights reserved. No part of this publication may be reproduced,
stored in a retrieval system, or transmitted, in any form or by
any means, electronic, mechanical, photocopying, recording, or
otherwise, without prior written permission from the publisher.

Library of Congress Cataloging-in-Publication data available upon request.

ISBN 1-56799-292-7

Editor: Tony Burgess
Consulting Editor: David Phillips
Art Director: Jeff Batzli
Designer: Kevin Ullrich
Photography Editor: Emilya Naymark

Color separations by Bright Arts (Singapore) Pte. Ltd.
Printed in China by Leefung-Asco Printers Ltd.

For bulk purchases and special sales, please contact:
Friedman/Fairfax Publishers
Attention: Sales Department
15 West 26th Street
New York, NY 10010
212/685-6610 FAX 212/685-1307

DEDICATION

I wish to dedicate this book to my family, and all of my students.
May they always quest for knowledge. Especially to my little son
in heaven, 'Baby Sam.'

CONTENTS

PREFACE

I never tire of reading about the American Civil War, and apparently I am not alone; nearly every year sees a new crop of books on this fascinating subject, and these books always find a ready audience. This is not surprising. The Civil War remains the most traumatic crisis that our nation has ever faced, and its effects continue to play a role in shaping our social and political landscape. To study the Civil War, to understand its causes and its effects, is to seek to understand the United States itself.

The Civil War is also, in many ways, our national loss of innocence. As Mark Nesbitt says in *Thirty-Five Days to Gettysburg*, "If the American Civil War began as a great celebration, it ended as one unbelievable funeral procession. Of the more than three million soldiers involved, a horrifying twenty percent died." Despite the lingering bitter resentments that the war left in its wake, by the end of it the United States was more firmly unified than ever before, bonded by the sheer fact of having survived an appalling

catastrophe together. This was tested in 1898, during the Spanish-American War, when the Spanish government sent secret messages to the southern states, hoping to re-kindle the resentment that after thirty-three years was still, in many people, close to the surface, a barely healed wound. But the Spanish were rebuffed in no uncertain terms. Resentment and hatred there might still be, but from that point on we were, for better or for worse, a single, unified nation.

This book is about the Civil War's leaders. Certainly there were many more leaders than the fourteen singled out for discussion in this volume, but here you will meet some of the most interesting and powerful characters to have participated in the Civil War. You'll learn about their triumphs and failures, their virtues and their weaknesses, and, if I've done my job, you will learn about how each of them, in all their human complexity, influenced and altered the course of the war.

—Bill Sell

By the summer of 1862, when this photograph was taken, it was clear that the Civil War was likely to be a prolonged conflict. Here, elements of the Federal Engineer Corps are building a corduroy road, made of logs laid side by side, in preparation for the muddy conditions of the coming winter.

INTRODUCTION

Despite the passage of nearly a century and a half, the Civil War remains the costliest war in American history, in terms of the total number of killed and wounded. Several factors contributed to the extreme bloodiness of the Civil War. Large armies fought using strategies and formations developed fifty years earlier. At the same time, weapons technology had advanced quickly, rendering the old tactics obsolete faster than generals could develop new ones.

The military and political leaders of this war, therefore, were faced with unprecedented challenges. In order to succeed, they had to be intelligent and adaptable, able to think on their feet and to inspire their subordinates. They had to be creative and open-minded, willing to discard the military wisdom of the past and to learn from their battlefield experiences. In addition, generals needed to be sensitive to the subtle nature of the political questions at stake, and to the ways in which battlefield successes and failures could result in political reverses.

This book is an excellent introduction for anyone interested in learning about the political and military leaders of the Union and the Confederacy. These men entered into the service of their respective governments at a time when political disagreements between the North and South had been deepening since the end of the Mexican War. As violent confrontations began to develop, people became more and more passionate in their beliefs. Many of the generals and politicians who had to choose sides faced a difficult decision, and loyalty to state and country were sorely tested. None of them entered into the conflict thoughtlessly or casually.

In this beautifully illustrated volume, Bill Sell presents biographical sketches of fourteen key leaders of both the Union and the Confederacy. *Leaders of the North and South* is arranged so that readers can compare the backgrounds, education, and leadership abilities of the men who ran the war. The two presidents, Lincoln and Davis, appear in these pages, as do the head field commanders and strategists, Grant and Lee. These and other leaders are evaluated in terms of the relative contribution that each had on the progress and outcome of the war, leaving readers with a balanced and thoughtful understanding of this crucial element of the Civil War.

Each side expected the Civil War to be brief and relatively bloodless, but it turned out to be a national tragedy of unprecedented scope. Here are the men whose talents, faults, and characters shaped and defined this historic conflict.

— David Phillips

During the winter, the normal miseries of war were augmented by the necessity of long marches through freezing mud. At least the Union soldiers depicted here were provided with decent cold-weather clothing; Confederate troops began running short of supplies very early in the war, and many were completely unprepared for winter conditions.

PART ONE

THE UNION

chapter 1

ABRAHAM LINCOLN
Embattled President

"This is a world of compensation; and he who would be no slave must consent to have no slave. Those who deny freedom to others deserve it not for themselves, and, under a just God, cannot long retain it."

—*Abraham Lincoln in a letter to H. L. Pierce, 1859.*

Abraham Lincoln is undoubtedly the single most enduring figure to emerge from the Civil War, and is generally agreed to have been the greatest president that the United States has ever had. During his life, however, and especially during his presidency, he was very far from being universally admired. Had he not been forced to deal with the greatest crisis that the country had ever faced, it is doubtful that he would now enjoy the reputation that he does.

Lincoln was born in extremely modest circumstances in a log cabin near Hodgenville, Kentucky, on February 12, 1809. His father, Thomas Lincoln, was a restless man, with no education or money, and throughout Abraham's early life the pioneer family moved about frequently.

Over the course of his childhood, Lincoln received barely one year of formal education, but it was enough to engage his remarkable intellectual curiosity. He became an avid reader at a very early age, traveling far and wide in search of books that he might borrow.

Although there has been much controversy regarding Lincoln's true feelings about the institution of slavery and about the reasons for which he eventually issued the Emancipation Proclamation, which led to the Thirteenth Amendment to the Constitution, there can be little doubt that he was sincere in his opposition to slavery on moral grounds. Much of his youth was spent among Baptists in rural Kentucky, who were generally hostile to slavery.

Young Lincoln worked for a while as a ferryman on the Ohio river, and at the age of nineteen he helped take a flatboat cargo to New Orleans. In this relatively cosmopolitan city, Lincoln encountered a manner of living previously wholly unknown to him.

In 1830 Lincoln's family moved to Indiana, where they yet again went through the pioneer routine of clearing wild land, building a log cabin, and beginning to grow meagre crops. That winter, however, the entire family came down with a severe fever, and Thomas Lincoln decided to move once again, back to Illinois. This time, however, Abraham did not accompany his family, having contracted to take another cargo to New Orleans. Thus began his life as an independent man.

On this second trip to New Orleans, Lincoln is supposed to have witnessed a slave auction, and the story goes that he said, "If I ever get a chance to hit that thing, I'll hit it hard." The story, however, is almost certainly apocryphal.

In 1831 Lincoln settled in New Salem, Illinois, a town that was undergoing a brief boom, thanks to the belief that the Sangamon river, on whose banks New Salem sat, would soon be made navigable for riverboats, making the town a major trading post. Lincoln gained the admiration of the roughest element of the community, a group known as the Clary's Grove Boys, when he threw their champion in a wrestling match. At the same time, however, his honesty, charm, and constant efforts at self-improvement so impressed the more reputable members of the community that he soon earned their respect as well. He became a member of the local debating society, and continued his studies of grammar and literature, developing an abiding love of Shakespeare and Robert Burns.

At this time Lincoln was employed as a clerk in a store owned by a trader named

PAGE 15: *Abraham Lincoln, photographed by Alexander Gardner in November 1863. In this photo, Lincoln conveys inner strength, and shows none of the stress that became evident in photographs made later in the war. ABOVE: Lincoln was seen by many as having realized the American dream: through hard work and honesty, he had progressed from manual labor to the presidency.*

Denton Offutt, but Offutt had been neglecting business and the store was on the verge of collapse. When the Black Hawk War broke out in Illinois in April 1832, Lincoln enlisted and was elected captain of his volunteer company. In one of history's more unusual coincidences, the officer who swore him in as captain was Jefferson Davis, later to become the president of the Confederate States of America.

After serving a total of eighty days in the armed service, during which time he did not see any fighting, Lincoln returned to New Salem, where he made his first foray into the field of politics by running for the state legislature. He was popular enough that he garnered nearly every vote in his own community, but he was not widely known outside of New Salem, and he ended up losing the election. He then decided to go into business, and bought a store on credit with a partner, but the store soon failed, leaving him deeply in debt. Over the next several years, his earnest efforts to pay off his accumulated debts were to earn him the nickname "Honest Abe."

In 1834, after having worked at a number of odd jobs, Lincoln was elected to the Illinois House of Representatives, where he soon discovered that he was extremely adept at political maneuvering and infighting. He was reelected in 1836, 1838, and 1840.

During these years, political alignments in the United States were in a state of flux, as the abolitionist movement began to gather force. When certain legislation denouncing antislavery agitation was before the House, Lincoln and his colleague Dan Stone defined their position by a written declaration that slavery was "founded on both injustice and bad policy, but that the promulgation of abo-

During the campaign of 1858, Lincoln addresses a procession that has halted in front of his home in Springfield, Illinois. He is the tall figure dressed in white standing at the right of the doorway.

ABOVE: Mary Todd Lincoln may have had a quick temper, but their happy marriage produced four children. RIGHT: After he won the presidential election of 1860, in which the Democratic party split into two factions over the issue of slavery, Lincoln is inaugurated at an unfinished Capital building.

litionist doctrines tends rather to increase than abate its evils." In this succinct statement, we may see clearly the position that Lincoln would hold all his life. He rejected slavery on moral grounds while at the same time recognizing that in practical terms the issue was extremely delicate and had to be dealt with cautiously.

While serving as a state legislator, Lincoln also worked as a lawyer, a profession that he continued until his election to the U.S. House of Representatives in 1846.

In 1842, Lincoln married Mary Todd. Despite her quick temper, instability, and vanity, the marriage appears to have been a happy one. Of their four children, only one, Robert Todd Lincoln, born in 1843, lived to maturity. After Lincoln's assissination, Mary

was so unbalanced by grief that at one time her son was forced to have her committed to a mental institution.

In 1846, after working for many years as a major voice in the Whig party, Lincoln was rewarded with his party's nomination as a candidate for Congress, winning the election handily over his Democratic opponent.

During his term in congress, Lincoln worked hard but did not distinguish himself. The Whig party, at this time, was a moderate voice against slavery, working out legislative compromises between the proslavery Democratic party and the radical abolitionists who were gaining ever more influence. Lincoln's ideas on slavery developed and deepened during this time, as he gained experience in dealing with this highly charged issue.

In 1848, after having laboured strenuously for the election of the Whig candidate for president, Zachary Taylor, Lincoln became disillusioned with politics when he did not receive a juicy patronage appointment as a reward for his efforts. He returned to Springfield, Illinois, his most recent home, where he devoted himself to the study of the law and literature.

In 1854, Lincoln returned to politics thanks to an event that, he declared, roused him as never before. It was the attempt, by a faction of the Democratic Party, to repeal certain elements of the Missouri Compromise, which had limited slavery to the states where it already existed. More mature, more intellectually developed, less interested in petty partisan politics, and driven by moral earnestness, Lincoln returned to the stump to campaign for the anti-slavery cause. In 1858, he ran against Stephen Douglas for the U.S. Senate, and although he eventually lost in a close election, the series of debates that he held with Douglas brought him national attention. Two years later he was able to finagle the presidential nomination

from the young Republican party, and when the Democratic party split over the issue of slavery, his election was assured.

As Lincoln took office, he faced an amazingly difficult task. Seven states had already seceded, and Jefferson Davis was sitting as Confederate president. Maryland, Kentucky, and Missouri were also debating secession.

Lincoln soon proved himself a poor administrator, appointing a cabinet that represented so many conflicting points of view that it was often impossible for its members to work together productively. At the same time, he gained considerable popularity for his warm wit, his engaging style, and his openness. The White House was open to all visitors, and he was eager to hear the views of his constituents. He soon came to be thought of as the people's president.

In 1861, when Confederate forces fired on Fort Sumter, beginning the Civil War, Lincoln took immediate control of the situation. As Congress was not in session, he was able to act unilaterally to requisition 75,000 troops from the states. Thenceforth, he retained complete control of the prosecution of the war, exercising a degree of personal power that no other president had ever before wielded. For this he was accused throughout the war of acting as a tyrant and a dictator. Partisan newspapers attacked him without mercy, calling him "a slangwhanging stump speaker," a "half-witted usurper," a "mole-eyed" monster with a "soul...of leather," "the present turtle at the head of government." Men of his own party openly called him "unfit," a "political coward," a "dictator," "timid and ignorant," "shattered, dazed, utterly foolish."

As the war dragged on, and as Lincoln failed to find a general who could successfully mobilize the Union's growing military resources to assault the Confederacy in earnest, he lost ever more political ground.

Confederate leaders in Charleston, South Carolina, demanded the surrender of Fort Sumter's Federal garrison in 1861. Lincoln refused to allow the surrender, and attempted to reinforce the garrison. The post was shelled very heavily, and was forced to surrender after suffering severe damage.

One of the generals in whom he had first placed a great deal of faith, but who ended up by disappointing him bitterly, George B. McClellan, was nominated by the Democratic party to run against Lincoln in the election of 1864. McClellan had his weaknesses as a candidate, not the least of which was that he was a pro-war candidate nominated by an anti-war party, but the threat to Lincoln was serious, because people were becoming exhausted with this terrible war that was taking so many lives with so little to show for the carnage. Furthermore, whereas the war had originally been fought only partly over the issue of slavery, after the Emancipation Proclamation and the subsequent passage of the Thirteenth Amendment, the general perception became that the North was fighting for the freedom of black men, a cause that was not such a powerful motivation for the majority of people in the North. Lincoln's

After the Battle of Antietam, Lincoln traveled the short distance to the village of Sharpsburg, Maryland, to review general strategy with George McClellan (not shown). The president's bodyguard, Allan Pinkerton, who founded the Pinkerton Detective Agency, is in civilian clothing at the left.

prospects improved immeasurably, however, when Ulysses S. Grant proved himself to be a general worthy of his new position in overall command of Union forces. When Grant drove Lee back into a defensive posture before Richmond, while General William Tecumseh Sherman invaded Georgia and captured Atlanta, it became clear to voters that the tide of the war was turning strongly in the Union's favor, and Lincoln's reelection was all but assured.

Once Sherman and Grant managed to squeeze between them the worn-out armies of Lee and Joseph Johnston, the war was quickly over. Lincoln was committed to establishing a just and lasting peace. He wanted to ensure civil rights for the freed slaves while easing the South back into the Union in a way that would minimize lasting resentments. He did not live to oversee the reconstruction of the South, however, for on April 14, 1865, John Wilkes Booth shot him in the back of the head at Ford's Theater, and he died the following day.

After his assassination, people all across the country began to realize what a man they had lost, and the public mourning that was displayed along the route of the train that took Lincoln's body back to Springfield, Illinois, was remarkable.

It is impossible to sum up concisely the tremendous influence and acheivements of a man who has acquired nearly mythical status in the American mind. Suffice it to say that had the United States not had him available at the time of its greatest trial, a man who knew how to blend political expediency with high moral purpose, and who had the passion and determination to see the crisis through to its conclusion, it would now be a very different country indeed. Edwin Stanton, his secretary of war, best expressed Lincoln's historic stature when, standing over the recently expired corpse, he said: "now he belongs to the ages."

ULYSSES S. GRANT

The Union's Best Soldier

"The art of war is simple enough. Find out where your enemy is. Get at him as soon as you can. Strike at him as hard as you can and as often as you can, and keep moving on."

—Ulysses S. Grant

Ulysses S. Grant was the best the North had to offer. He was probably not the most brilliant of its leaders, and he certainly had his faults, but the man was not afraid of a fight, and he had a gift for leading troops.

Grant was at the lowest point in his career when the war started. He had failed in business, failed at farming, and failed in the military. In the war he saw an opportunity to redeem some of those past failures. He was, after all, a graduate of the United States Military Academy, and since the War Department was short of personnel, he was confident that it would accept the offer of his services. So this son of an Ohio fur skinner jumped at the chance of a new start in life, and was assigned to the western theater of war, where the groundwork was to be estab-lished for the final, successful campaign against the South.

Ulysses Grant was a man of humble ori-gins, and humility followed him through his military and public career as well. He was not one for pomp and show, and when later in the war he was elevated to the highest rank, he never displayed it in his uniform or appearance. He was a man of direct con-frontation. His wife Julia later told a story that took place when they were courting. The couple attended her cousin's wedding in the spring of the year. She was riding behind Ulysses on horseback when they came to a swollen stream. Rather than search for a safer place to cross, Grant spurred his horse and plunged right in, scaring his fiancée half to death. That was the way he was; he would

never take a long way around when the direct approach was the shortest.

In February of 1862, Grant pleaded with his superior General Henry Halleck to let him take troops down into Tennesee and try to capture some Confederate forts on the Tennesee River. Halleck was suspicious of Grant; an enterprising and successful subordinate might threaten his own reputation. He was glad to send Grant off on a dangerous mission in the freezing rain, knowing that if Grant failed he would no longer be a threat politically, and that if he was successful, Halleck could reap the benefits as well.

Grant saw an advantage that could be gained for Northern arms through the use of the North's original plan, which was called the Anaconda plan. Grant would use the navigable rivers of the region as transportation routes, allowing him to move his forces quickly into areas where the Confederates would have to march to oppose him. The use of the western rivers as lines of communication offered another advantage. The ships and boats of the navy could be utilized both as trasport and as mobile fortresses that could fire heavy shells into defender's positions when called for.

Fort Henry and Fort Donelson, on the Tennessee-Kentucky border, were the first targets of Grant's strategy. Andrew Foote's gunboats steamed up near Fort Henry and shelled the low-lying fortifications into submission without the use of a ground attack. Confederate troops evacuated and moved to Fort Donelson, and were just as quickly followed by Grant's men.

The gunboats were less successful at Fort Donelson, as the fort's heavy batteries were placed in higher positions, and many of Foote's shells passed harmlessly over the defender's heads; meanwhile, plunging fire from the fort struck directly into the gunboats. This unfair contest ended when Foote's vessels withdrew.

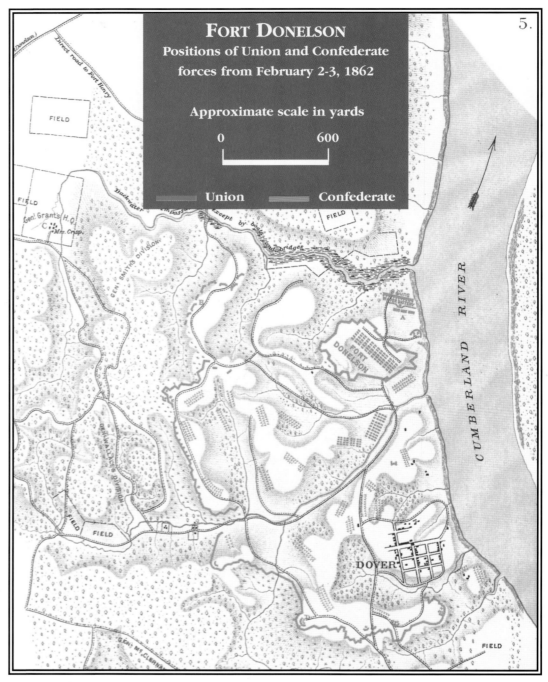

PAGE 23: Ulysses S. Grant had been a failure in the military as well as in several attempted civilian professions. The Civil War gave him an opportunity to rebuild his personal and professional life, and he was to become one of the first practitioners of modern warfare. ABOVE: Fort Donelson was a major Confederate bastion that was designed to defend against waterborne attacks into Tennessee. Strong defensive works did little good, however, as the fort was commanded by two very poor commanders. Grant accepted the "unconditional surrender" of the doomed fort from one of his best friends in the pre-war army, Simon Bolivar Buckner.